BASIC / NOT BORING

PHONICS & WORD SKILLS

Grades 2-3

Inventive Exercises to Sharpen Skills and Raise Achievement

Series Concept & Development
by Imogene Forte & Marjorie Frank
Exercises by Laurie Grupé

Incentive Publications, Inc.
Nashville, Tennessee

About the cover:
Bound resist, or tie dye, is the most ancient known method of fabric surface design. The brilliance of the basic tie dye design on this cover reflects the possibilities that emerge from the mastery of basic skills.

Illustrated by Kathleen Bullock
Cover art by Mary Patricia Deprez, dba Tye Dye Mary®
Cover design by Marta Drayton, Joe Shibley, and W. Paul Nance
Edited by Anna Quinn

ISBN 0-86530-391-6

PRINTED IN THE UNITED STATES OF AMERICA

TABLE OF CONTENTS

Appendix

CELEBRATE BASIC LANGUAGE SKILLS

Basic does not mean boring! There is certainly nothing dull about . . .

    . . . exploring the world in a submarine or a helicopter

    . . . traveling forward into space or backward into time

    . . . stalking a wild boar, the abominable snowman, or Bigfoot

    . . . searching for pirate's treasure or underground caves

    . . . surfing Australia's Great Reef or hiking China's Great Wall

    . . . fighting a wild bull, taming a lion, or confronting a fire-breathing dragon

    . . . visiting the world's highest and lowest, coldest and hottest spots

    . . . riding a camel, an elephant, or a giraffe through deserts and grasslands

These are just some of the adventures students can explore as they celebrate basic word skills. The idea of celebrating the basics is just what it sounds like—enjoying and improving the skills of reading and using words. Each page invites young learners to try a high-interest, visually appealing exercise that will sharpen one specific word skill. This is not just an ordinary fill-in-the-blanks way to learn. These exercises are fun and surprising. Students will do the useful work of practicing word skills while they enjoy unusual adventures with the Worldwide Adventure Company.

The book can be used in many ways:

- to review or practice a skill with one student
- to sharpen the skill with a small or large group
- to start off a lesson on a particular skill
- to assess how well a student has mastered a skill

Each page has directions that are written simply. It is intended that an adult be available to help students read the information on the page, if needed. In most cases, the pages will be used best as a follow-up to a skill that has already been taught. The pages are excellent tools for immediate reinforcement of a concept.

As your students take on the challenges of these adventures with words, they will grow! And as you watch them check off the basic language skills they've strengthened, you can celebrate with them.

The Skills Test

Use the skills test beginning on page 58 as a pretest and/or a post-test. This will help you check the students' mastery of basic language skills and prepare them for success on achievement tests.

SKILLS CHECKLIST
PHONICS & WORD SKILLS, GRADES 2-3

✔	SKILL	PAGE(S)
	Identify and read beginning and ending consonants	10, 11, 13–19
	Identify and read medial consonants	11, 12
	Identify and read beginning and ending consonant blends	13–17
	Identify and read beginning and ending digraphs	16, 17
	Identify double consonants	18
	Put words in alphabetical order	19
	Identify and read short vowels	20, 21
	Identify and read long vowels	20, 22, 23, 27, 28, 29
	Identify and read long vowels with silent e	23
	Identify double vowels	24
	Identify and read various vowel combinations	25–29
	Distinguish between y as a vowel and as a consonant	30
	Identify and read words with silent letters	31
	Use phonics to read whole words	32
	Identify and read inflectional endings	33
	Identify and use common prefixes	34, 36
	Identify and use common suffixes	35, 36
	Identify and use common root words	37, 38
	Determine syllables in words	39, 40
	Identify and read contractions	41, 42
	Identify and form compound words	43
	Discriminate between words that look similar	44
	Identify and discriminate between homonyms	45, 46
	Identify and read proper nouns	47
	Identify and read plural nouns	48
	Identify and read possessive nouns	49
	Recognize and use synonyms	50, 52
	Recognize and use antonyms	51, 52
	Recognize and use words with multiple meanings	53
	Classify words according to meaning and use	54
	Learn new words	55, 56
	Form words from other words	57

PHONICS & WORD SKILLS

Grades 2-3

Skills Exercises

The Adventure Company

Choose Your Adventure!

The signs tell about some exciting adventures.
Look at all the signs.
   Circle the **beginning consonants or blends** with red.
   Circle the **ending consonants or blends** with blue.

Welcome to the Worldwide Adventure Company. We have thrilling adventures for everyone.

Sounds good.

Unusual Adventures!

Fight a fire-breathing dragon.
Ride a barrel over Niagara Falls.
Look inside meat-eating plants.
Steer a boat around icebergs.
Surf a monstrous wave.
Rocket through the solar system.
Follow a rare mountain gorilla.
Travel into the past.
Explore deep, dark caves.

Far Off Adventures!

Sahara Desert
Great Wall of China
Deep Amazon Rain Forest
Beautiful Swiss Alps
High Himalayan Mountains
Great Coral Reef
Wild Alaska Wilderness

Name _____

Use with page 11.

Beginning, Middle, & Ending Consonants

Basic Skills/Phonics & Word Skills 2-3

Choose Your Adventure, cont.

Search for consonants or consonant blends in the middle of words.
Circle middle consonants or blends with green.

Most Unusual Places.....

The coldest spot on Earth
The hottest spot on Earth
The highest spot on Earth
The lowest spot on Earth
The Earth's biggest desert
The Earth's longest caves

Most Exciting Rides.......

Ferris wheel   helicopter
tornado   parachute
camel   elephant
rocket   time machine
giraffe   bucking bronco

The Most Dangerous Adventures.....

Swamp Cruising
Bullfighting
Lion Taming
Alligator Wrestling
Moose Tracking
Chasing the Wild Boar
Tracking the Mountain Gorilla
Hurricane Watching
Log Rolling
Stalking Bigfoot

Name _____

Use with page 10.

(11)

Beginning, Middle, & Ending Consonants

A Bumpy Camel Ride

When you read about the camel ride, you will see that some words are missing. Choose a word from the **Word Box** to fill in each blank.

Look for the consonants in the middle of the words.

Circle the middle consonants. (There are two in the middle of some words!)

Adventure # 1
Ride a furry Bactrian camel through the grasslands of Asia. Bring your camera, and be prepared for a bumpy, lumpy ride!

Giddy-up

The _____ has two humps.

You will have fun _____ this _____ creature!

You can_____ yourself right between the two humps and hold on tight.

The Bactrian camel has wide flat feet to keep it from _____ into the soft ground.

Bring _____for warm and cool temperatures.

The grassland home of the camel is sometimes hot like a _____.

At night, it gets close to _____.

On your adventure you may see a suslik, which is an animal like a _____. He digs in _____ or tunnels.

Look out for a poisonous _____!

He is the _____ desert snake!

WORD BOX

viper	desert
camel	freezing
riding	burrows
clothing	fuzzy
sinking	settle
rodent	largest

Name _____

Middle Consonants

Reptile Races

> Which one do <u>You</u> think is the fastest?

Adventure # 2

Travel to the desert to watch a race between the Tricky Lizard and the Sticky-Tongued Snake. Which one will get the yummy first prize?

The Tricky Lizard can only follow words that begin with the **tr** blend. Color his path to the prize **green**.

The Sticky-Tongued Snake can only follow words that begin with the **st** blend. Color his path to the prize **yellow**.

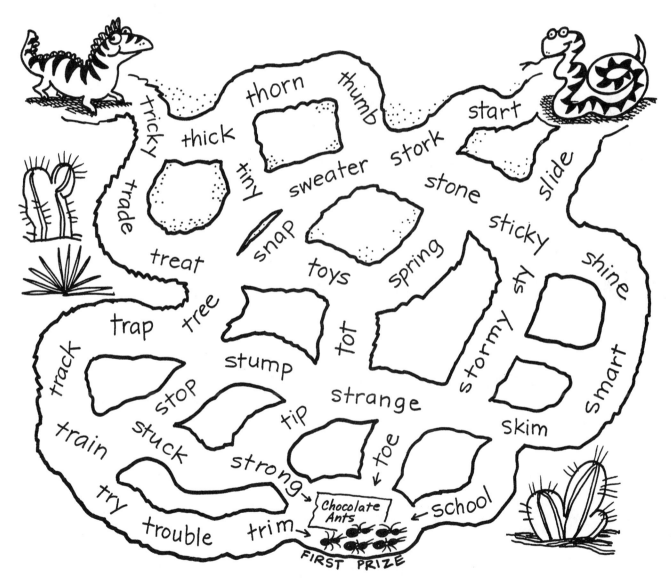

thorn thumb thick tiny sweater stork start slide stone sticky tricky trade treat snap toys spring sty stormy shine trap tree tot smart track stump skim stop strange tip toe train stuck strong school try trouble trim

Chocolate Ants
FIRST PRIZE

Which animal has the shortest path? (Circle one.)   **snake   lizard**

Name _____

Consonant Blends

A Low-Down Place

The trench is filled with **s** blends that can be used to begin words.

Make a word by writing an **s** blend at the beginning of each word on the right.

Adventure # 3
You bring the camera! We'll bring the submarine! You can explore the lowest spot on Earth!

sk

squ

sc

sw

st

sl

sm

sn

sp

The lowest spot ever reached is the Marianas Trench in the Pacific Ocean. It is 36,000 feet below sea level!

The Adventure Co. Submarine

1. _____ ick

2. _____ ile

3. _____ arf

4. _____ at

5. _____ iff

6. _____ lrrel

7. _____ ate

8. _____ ray

9. _____ ail

10. _____ im

11. _____ oon

12. _____ lp

13. _____ unk

14. _____ eep

15. _____ ash

16. _____ oop

17. _____ ing

18. _____ op

Name _____

S Blends

Copyright ©1998 by INCENTIVE PUBLICATIONS, Inc., Nashville, TN.
Basic Skills/Phonics & Word Skills 2-3

A High-in-the-Sky Place

The mountain is filled with **l** and **r** blends that can be used to begin words.

Make a word by writing one of the blends at the beginning of each word.

1. _____own
2. _____ue
3. _____ite
4. _____ing
5. _____og
6. _____oat
7. _____ass
8. _____ain
9. _____ippery
10. _____ate
11. _____eek
12. _____y
13. _____ip
14. _____ide
15. _____ong
16. _____ow
17. _____ick
18. _____op

The Adventure Company

Mt. Everest, in Nepal, is 29,028 feet tall. It is called the world's highest place.

bl
cr
pl
cl
gl
fr
sl
br
dr
fl
wr
tr
pr

Name _____

Through the Iceberg Maze

Adventure #5

Bring warm clothes and be ready for a challenge.
We're heading across an icy ocean, and we have a lot of icebergs to dodge.

Color icebergs blue if the words begin or end with these digraphs: **sh, th,** or **ch.**

Draw a path across the water that passes near these icebergs.

wing

chip

bush

mink

math

skin

sock

chin

stuck

thumb

scale

jump

milk

shop

catch

brisk

worst

sang

wish

risk

birch

duck

Draw a circle around these beginnings and endings:
ng   nk   ck
lk   st
mp   sk
sc

scoot

with

The Adventure Co.
Sea Craft

Name _____

Over the Edge

The words in the barrel were shaken up so much that they have split apart.

Use a crayon or marker to circle the parts that belong together.

Write the words on the lines.

Adventure # 6
What a thrill to ride a waterfall!
Some people do it in a raft or canoe.
Others can do it in a barrel.
Hang on tight, and prepare to get tossed around.

1. _____

2. _____   6. _____

3. _____   7. _____

4. _____   8. _____

5. _____   9. _____

Name _____

Consonant Blends & Digraphs

The Super Ferris Wheel

The words on the seats have double consonants in them.

Circle the double consonants in each word.

Then choose the best word to fit in each sentence.

sunny

chilly

cotton

terrific

1. I was beginning to _____ about this ride.

2. We're glad it is a bright _____ day at the fair.

3. The wind is a little _____ way up high.

arrow

funny

4. I should have worn something warmer than a _____ shirt.

5. We started to _____ when we got near the top.

worry

puddle

6. Look! Someone is having a _____ right here at the fair!

7. It's _____ how small people look down below.

furry

giggle

8. This was an exciting, _____ ride!

wedding

Name _____

Double Consonants

Snorkeling the Great Reef

Draw a line to connect the names in alphabetical order.
Then you will see another sea creature.
What is it?

starfish

tuna

squid

shark

sponge

oyster

goby

frog fish

jellyfish

urchin

octopus

eel

anemone

dolphin

limpet

clam

zebra fish

crab   lobster   manatee

Name _____

Alphabetizing

Deep in the Rain Forest

The rain forest is filled with unusual plants and lost vowels.

Write the missing vowels into the words in the picture.

Then write the first vowel from words 1, 3, 5, and 7 into the blanks in number 11.

You'll spell the name of a very long jungle animal.

Name _____

The Bullfight

When the bullfighter enters the ring, he must go carefully toward the bull.
Color a path for him that follows the words with short vowel sounds.

run sun bull red

crowd cheer trip

fear

cape fight fall

careful pay snort shoe rip cone

skip cloak

horns mud hop crazy

rosy flop

cheer flick

able stop

Adventure # 10
Are you really brave
enough for this?
Fighting an angry bull
is a tough job.
Get your red cape
ready, and be fast on
your feet!

Name _____

Short Vowels

Clowning Around

Follow all the directions.
Then circle all the words with long vowel sounds.

1. Draw a bow in the clown's hair.

2. Draw a smile on her face.

3. Draw a kite in the air.

4. Draw a string from the kite to her hand.

5. Draw an ice cream cone in her other hand.

6. Color her nose red.

7. Color her cape green.

8. Draw a rose on each shoe.

9. Draw a cupcake in her pocket.

10. Draw a balloon for her pet.

Color the clown carefully.

Name _____

Lion-Sized Thrills

Help make the lion's cage strong enough to hold the lion.

Color the squares in the cage where the words have long vowels with a **silent e** at the end (such as **cage, bite, bones,** and **cute**).

If you find at least 20, you'll keep the lion tamer safe and healthy.

Adventure # 12
Here's a really thrilling circus adventure! Learn how the lion tamer tames a fierce lion.

sting	tame	drool	beet	drone	paws	rate	cage	shop	help	fun	cake
page	whip	tooth			stale	furry	smile	maul	dine	boot	
slope	door	bee	ate		mate	tail	claws	page	lock	key	
sea	cape	roar			June	sneer	cone	chair	white	door	
rose	black	sleep		ape	plate	sharp	yelp	twist	rage		

Name _____

Moose Tracking

Adventure # 13
Tracking the wild moose is quite a skill. You can learn to follow moose in the north woods of Canada and Alaska. No shooting is allowed—except with a camera!

As you read about the moose, look for words with double vowels.

Write these words on the lines. Write each word only once. How many different words can you find?

I can't see anything!

The Adventure Company Jeep

There is a big, goofy-looking moose on the loose in the deep woods of northern Canada. Look! Can you see his trail of moose prints? What huge feet he has! The track of each foot is six inches long. He needs these large feet when he moves through cool pools and ponds looking for food. He likes to feed on plants and never eats toadstools or beetles. The moose is very quiet, so he is hard to find. This moose lives in Canada. Moose live in Alaska, too! But this moose would probably never live in a zoo. He would rather be free!

List the words that you found.
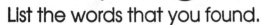

1. _____   8. _____   15. _____
2. _____   9. _____   16. _____
3. _____   10. _____   17. _____
4. _____   11. _____   18. _____
5. _____   12. _____   19. _____
6. _____   13. _____   20. _____
7. _____   14. _____

There are ____ different words with double vowels.

More tourists.

Name _____

Rhino Watching

Read about the rhino and his bird friends.
Look for words that have vowel combinations
that give a **long e** sound.
(This sound can be made by **e, ee, ie,** or **ea.**)
Circle the words that have a **long e** sound.

Adventure # 14
Come to Africa to watch
the great rhinoceros.
You'll find out that the rhino
has some important friends.

The rhinoceros is an odd-looking beast that is said to be
related to early dinosaurs. These days, there are not many
rhinos left in Africa. Some hunters seek them out and kill
them to take their large horns.

Their friends, the egrets (pronounced ee-grets), come in
flocks to sit on the backs of the rhinos and other large
animals. The egrets sit on the animals' backs and wait for
them to kick up insects with their feet. Then the egrets
quickly fly down to eat up the insects. This is a good
friendship, because the birds get a meal and the rhinos get
rid of bothersome insects.

Name _____

A Helicopter Flight

Adventure # 15
Get on board our Adventure helicopter!
You'll have the most exciting ride.
We'll follow the crow through the clouds to his lunch.
Everywhere he goes, we'll go, too!

Color the clouds with words having the sound made by **ow** in the word **crow**.

Draw a path for the crow that follows those clouds.

down

clown

tow

town

low

crown

know

brown

plow

cow

mow   how

show

growl

grow   now

prowl   snow   flow

Name _____

Meet the Meat Eaters

Meat-eating plants give off sweet-smelling, sticky nectar.

The smell attracts insects and other small creatures.

The sticky stuff keeps them from getting away!

Adventure # 16
Visit meat-eating plants around the world!
But keep your fingers in your pockets!

Use the vowel combinations in the plants to finish the words before the plant snaps shut!

1. p____n   10. m____l

2. c____ght   11. p____son

3. fr____ndly   12. retr____t

4. d____dly   13. m____th

5. ____t   14. gl____

6. h____t   15. h____rs

7. m____t   16. t____ch

8. ____chl   17. ab____t

9. b____t   18. ag____nst

Don't worry! These plants don't eat humans.

Name _____

Vowel Combinations

Fire Danger!

Take a trip into the long-ago past to battle a fire-breathing dragon. Get into your knight's metal suit, and don't forget to bring a sword!

To tame the dragon, circle all the vowels or vowel combinations that make a **long a** sound (such as in **tame**).

Hint: look for **ai, ey, ay,** and **a with a silent e** at the end of the word!

Fire!

Rules for Fighting a Dragon

1. Don't expect the dragon to be playful.
2. Take a sharp sword.
3. Don't be afraid.
4. Don't step on its tail.
5. Wave your sword wildly.
6. Aim straight for its heart.
7. Shout, "Hey! Go away!"
8. Escape before it's too late.

Name _____

Hurricane Watch

Solve each riddle with a word that has something to do with a storm.
Each word has a vowel combination of **ea, ai, ou,** or **oa.**

Adventure # 18

Hurricane Matilda is storming in.
We can watch the storm, but not from the boat.
We'll get to shore and find a safe place for watching.

Riddle 1

Get me out of the water
When the wind starts to blow.
Row me right to the shore,
And don't be slow!

I am a _____.
(I rhyme with "float.")

Riddle 3

Don't play here today
With your shovel and pail!
You'll get swept out to sea
And get pounded with hail.

I am the _____.
(I rhyme with "peach.")

Riddle 2

We're crashing waves.
We toss ships around.
We wash over beaches
And cover the ground.

Our sound is _____.
(It rhymes with "crowd.")

Riddle 4

I pour from the skies
And drench the land.
I blow in your windows
And soak into the sand.

I am the _____.
(I rhyme with "pane.")

Name _____

Yodel with a Yeti

Adventure # 19

Come hiking in the high Himalayan Mountains!
Old stories called legends say that a great, white creature can be seen there.
He's called a Yeti (or an abominable snowman).
You also might hear some yodeling in the mountains. (Is it the Yeti?!!)
You can even learn to yodel yourself.

Yodel-lay-dee-hoo!

Yodel-lady back at you.

yes   try   Yeti
today   lucky
yodeled   Yelled
yellow
easily   Yummy   snowy
fly   yank   silly
yikes!

The words on the mountain all have at least one **y**.
Sometimes **y** is a consonant, such as in **yet** or **yell.**
Sometimes **y** is a vowel, such as in **spy, key, stay,** or **funny.**
When **y** is a vowel, it helps make a **long a, long i,** or **long e** sound.
Write the words in the correct place below.
You will need to write one word in both places.

Words with **y** as a consonant: Words with **y** as a vowel:

_____   _____   _____   _____

_____   _____   _____   _____

_____   _____   _____   _____

_____   _____

Name _____

Copyright ©1998 by Incentive Publications, Inc., Nashville, TN.
Basic Skills/Phonics & Word Skills 2-3

Stalk a Sasquatch

Adventure # 20

It is said that a big hairy creature with huge feet stalks the woods of the Northwest United States. Join the searchers for the Sasquatch (also known as Bigfoot).
You must walk in silence.
Listen for the sound of big feet walking.

Color the footprints that contain silent letters.

This will show you the path to follow.

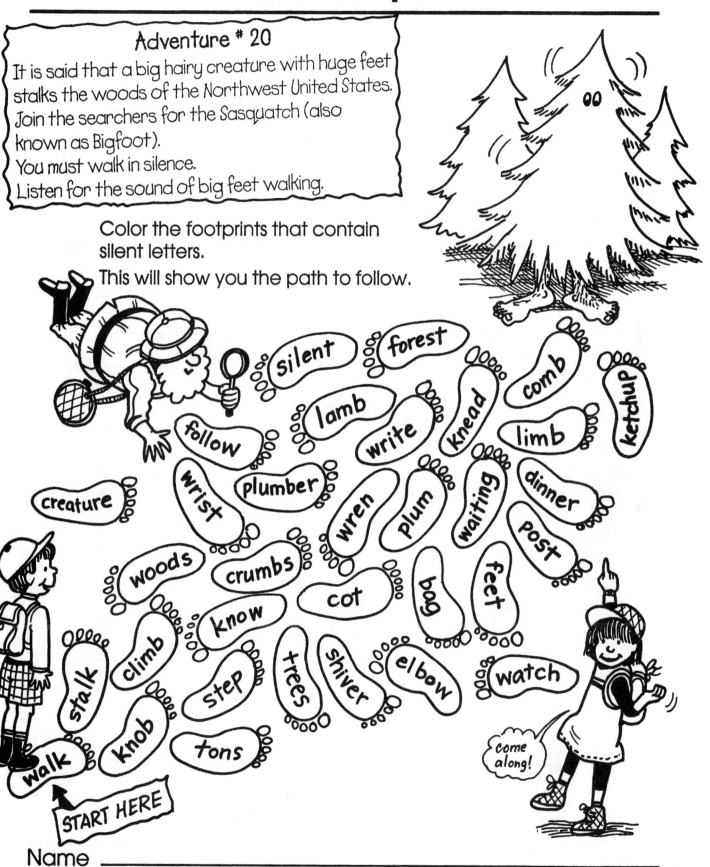

Name _____

Silent Letters

Hunt for Pirate's Treasure

Adventure # 21
Bring a shovel and a sack for treasure. We'll provide the map! Take a trip to the deserted Island of the Bones and dig for pirate's treasure.

What is in the treasure chest?
Look for words in the puzzle that name things that could be inside the chest. Circle any possible "treasures" you find.

(Words can be left to right, right to left, up and down, or down and up!)

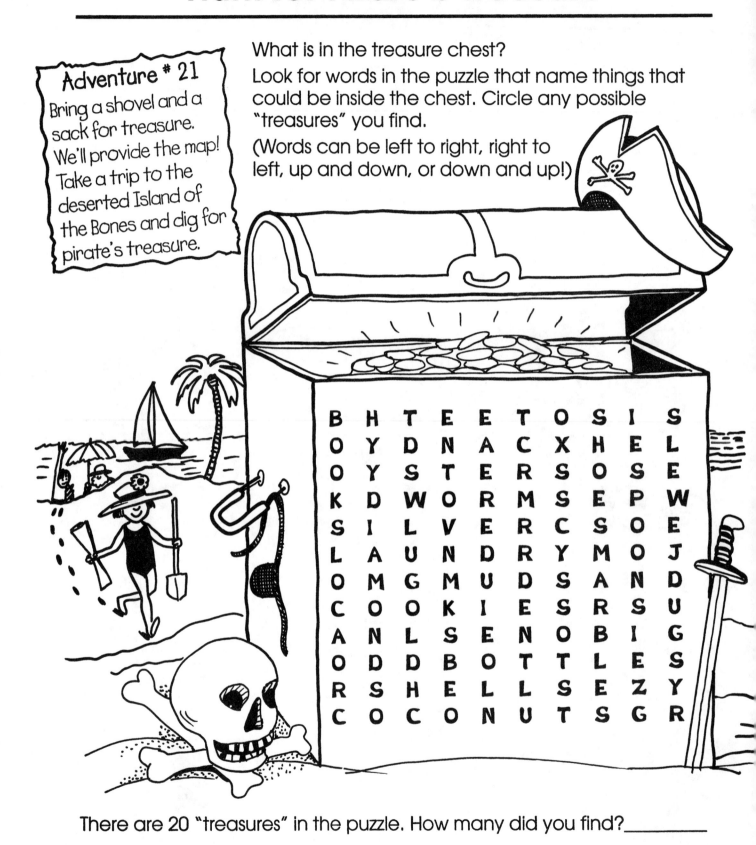

There are 20 "treasures" in the puzzle. How many did you find?_____

Name _____

Use Phonics to Read Whole Words

The Sea Turtle Races

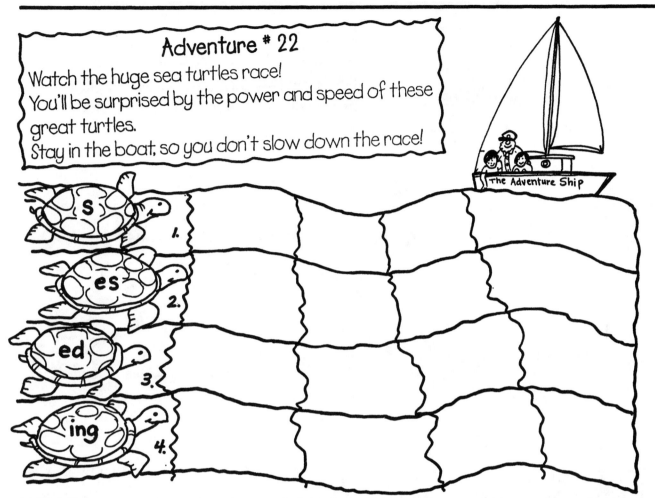

Adventure # 22
Watch the huge sea turtles race!
You'll be surprised by the power and speed of these great turtles.
Stay in the boat, so you don't slow down the race!

The Adventure Ship

Write the correct ending in each blank in the sentences. Use **s, es, ed,** or **ing.**

Each time you use an ending, color one part of its lane.

1. Will you be watch_____ the race today?

2. Leather-back turtles have weigh_____ up to 1500 pounds.

3. Turtles have thick heavy legs for walk_____.

4. Some turtles have liv_____ to be 100 years old!

5. Who shout_____ the loudest during the race?

6. We have been wait_____ a long time for the race.

7. Turtle number one trick_____ them every year.

8. I pick_____ the winner!

Which turtle gets the farthest? _____

Name _____

The Big Jump

Adventure # 23

Unpack your parachute, and get ready for the jump of your life! Follow all the safety rules.

Finish the words by adding one of the prefixes from the parachute. Each time you use a prefix, color its section. Be sure to color each section a different color.

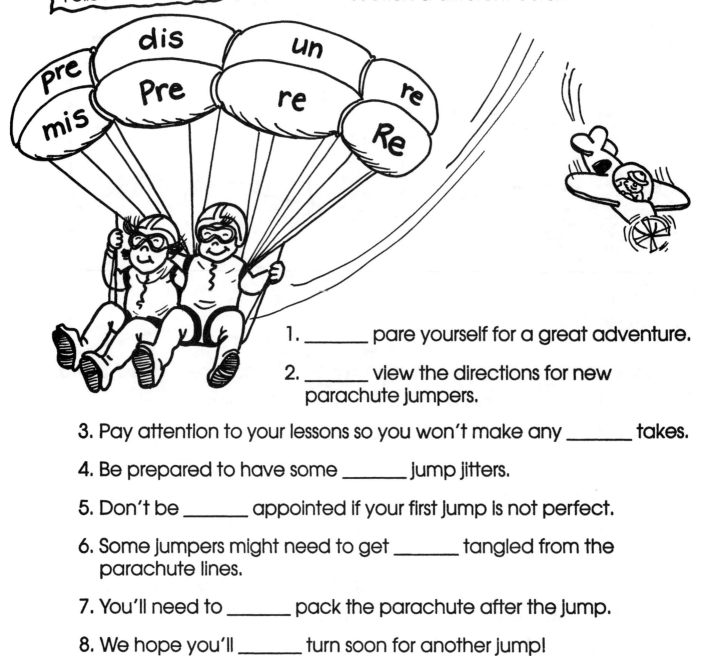

pre
mis
dis
Pre
un
re
re
Re

1. _____ pare yourself for a great adventure.

2. _____ view the directions for new parachute jumpers.

3. Pay attention to your lessons so you won't make any _____ takes.

4. Be prepared to have some _____ jump jitters.

5. Don't be _____ appointed if your first jump is not perfect.

6. Some jumpers might need to get _____ tangled from the parachute lines.

7. You'll need to _____ pack the parachute after the jump.

8. We hope you'll _____ turn soon for another jump!

Name _____

Log Rolling on the River

Adventure # 24

The slippery, rolling logs are the only way across the Raging Rapids River. The river is deep and cold, and it moves fast. Watch your step!

Choose the correct suffix to complete each word in the sentences.

Use the suffixes in the box at the bottom of the page.

Each time you finish a word, color that log.

1. The logs are the only poss_____ way to cross the river.

2. Choose the logs wise_____ .

3. Don't be care_____ as you cross.

4. The rushing waters are very danger_____ .

5. The water is more power_____ than you might think.

6. It would be fool_____ to think this is easy.

7. It is import_____ to move quick___ .

8. Show your friendli_____ by offering help to someone else.

9. Is this a good way to spend your vaca_____ ?

10. There will be much excite_____ when you get across.

ment	ous	ness	less	ant
ful	ly	ible	ish	tion

Name _____

Visit a Desert Hotel

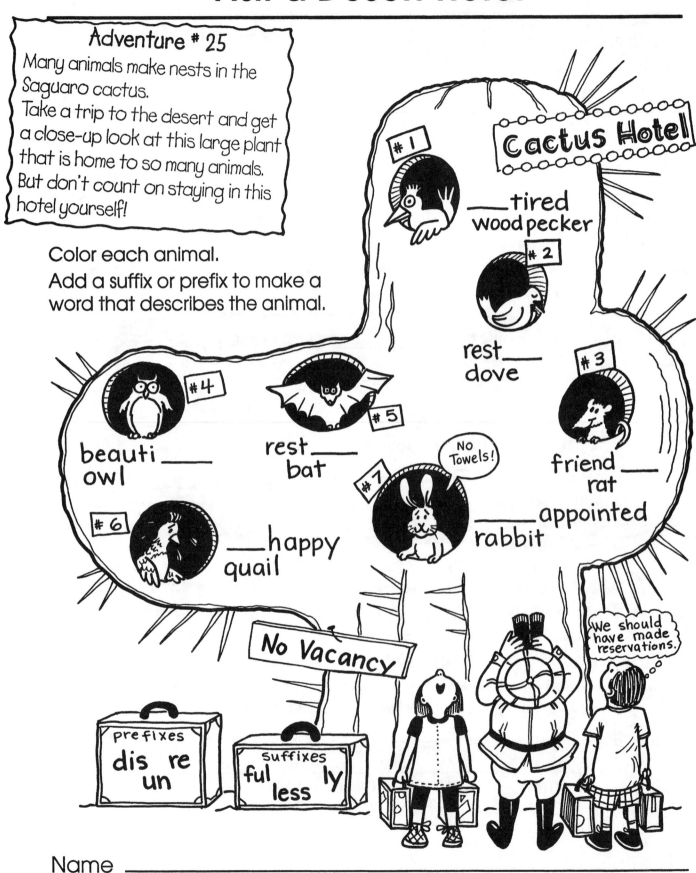

Adventure # 25

Many animals make nests in the Saguaro cactus.
Take a trip to the desert and get a close-up look at this large plant that is home to so many animals.
But don't count on staying in this hotel yourself!

Color each animal.

Add a suffix or prefix to make a word that describes the animal.

Cactus Hotel

#1 ____tired woodpecker

#2 rest____ dove

#3 friend____ rat

____appointed rabbit

#4 beauti____ owl

#5 rest____ bat

#6 ____happy quail

#7 No Towels!

No Vacancy

We should have made reservations.

prefixes
dis re
un

suffixes
ful ly
less

Name _____

Nighttime Snooping

A **root word** is a word that was there before prefixes or suffixes were added.
Look at the bold word in each of these sentences about nocturnal animals.
Decide what the root word is.
Write it on the line.

> **Adventure # 26**
> In Australia, there are many animals that stay awake all night.
> These animals are called nocturnal.
> Sneak up and watch them carefully, because not all of them are friendly!

1. The platypus is such an **unusual** animal. _____

2. Koala bears have **disappeared** from many areas. _____

3. The **poisonous** leaves of the eucalyptus tree do not harm koalas. _____

4. **Quietly** the desert shrew moves through the desert. _____

5. The Tasmanian devil is the **strangest** animal. _____

6. A marsupial mouse lemur sleeps **peacefully** all day. _____

7. Australia is home to some of the **largest** bats. _____

8. It's **unbelievable** how possums can spend so much time upside-down! _____

9. A Victoria koala lives in the **coldest** part of Australia. _____

10. Stay around for daylight, and watch the **powerful** kangaroos jumping. _____

Name _____

Root Words

Rodeo Ride

Read the word at the top of each group. Draw a lasso around the word that is the correct root word.

Remember: A **root word** is the word without any prefixes or suffixes added to it.

1. unstoppable
stop   able
unstop
stoppable

2. dangerous
danger
dan
dang

3. working
or
work
king

I'm as skillful with a lasso as a real cowgirl.

4. disagreeable
disagree
agreeable
agree   dis

5. blameless
am less blame

6. finest
fine fin nest

This bronco is full of wildness !

7. neighborhood
neigh bor
neighbor

snort snort

8. careful
full are care

I hope I don't mistakenly lasso myself !

9. untamed
un   tame
tamed   tam

10. unfriendliness
unfriendly   friendly
friendliness   friend

Name _____

A Swamp Cruise

Read all the words the characters are saying.
Pay attention to the number of syllables in the words.
Write one word on each line in the boxes below.

Adventure # 28
Cruise through the darkest swamp in the United States. Stop and wrestle an alligator. We hope you don't lose any arms or legs!

Welcome to Mosquito Swamp.
Don't fall out of the canoe, little explorers.
You might lose your hat in the river.
This wild alligator has dangerous teeth.
Taming him would be an impossibility!
Perhaps we should exit the swamp now.

Don't you want to wrestle?

one-syllable words:	two-syllable words:	three-syllable words:
_____	_____	_____
_____	_____	_____
_____	_____	_____
_____	_____	_____

Write a word with four syllables. _____

Write a word with six syllables. _____

Name _____

Tornado Alert!

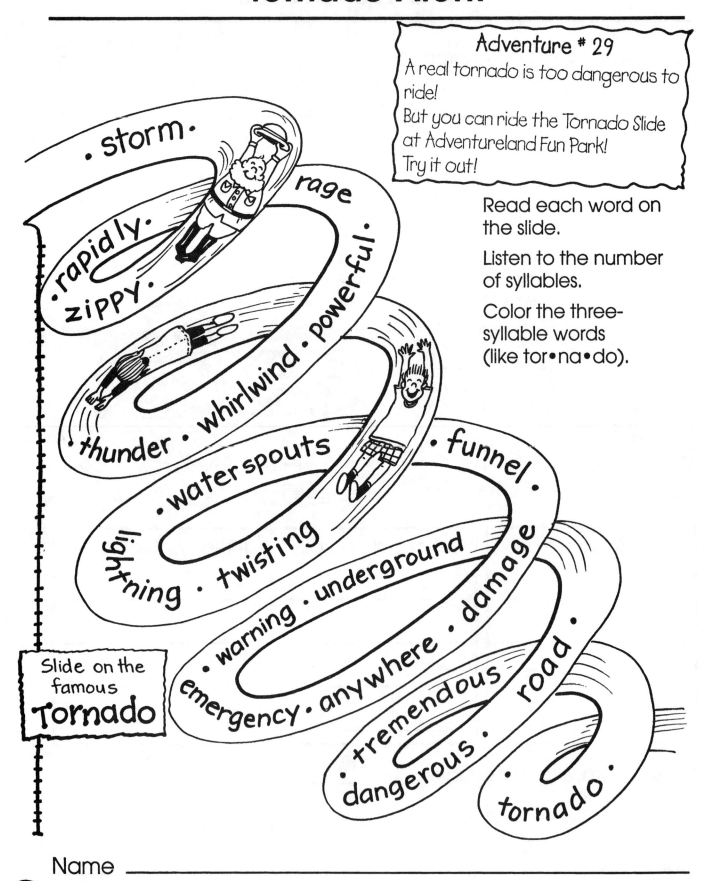

Adventure # 29

A real tornado is too dangerous to ride!
But you can ride the Tornado Slide at Adventureland Fun Park!
Try it out!

Read each word on the slide.

Listen to the number of syllables.

Color the three-syllable words (like tor•na•do).

• storm •

rage

rapidly •

• zippy •

powerful •

• whirlwind •

• thunder •

• waterspouts

lightning • twisting

• funnel •

warning • underground

emergency • anywhere • damage

• tremendous

dangerous •

road

• tornado •

Slide on the famous **Tornado**

Name _____

Volcanic Visit

Join our group of volcano-watchers!
See, hear, and feel the rumbles and eruptions!
Don't worry, we won't take you onto the mountain.

Each sentence has two words that can form a contraction.
Color the matching contraction in the puzzle.
What word appears? _____

don't	be	you'll	weave	couldn't	we've	isn't	there	shouldn't	they're	art	we'll
is	you're	who's		aren't					your	you've	

Ka

1. This volcano is not Mt. St. Helens.

2. Who is living near the active volcano?

3. The last visitors could not find the crater.

4. Many volcanoes are not finished changing.

5. We hope you are bringing a lunch with you.

6. You should not hike on an erupting volcano.

7. We will stay away from any lava flows.

8. They are getting too close to the side of the volcano!

9. You have found a vent at the side of the volcano.

10. We have seen some amazing sites at this volcano.

11. We do not know where the magma chamber is located.

12. You will enjoy hiking on the volcano when it stops acting up.

Name _____

Go Spelunking!

Adventure # 31
Go spelunking in the world's longest cave. (Spelunking is exploring caves.) Come to Mammoth Caves in Kentucky for an underground thrill. Bring your flashlight!

In each sentence below, combine the two words in **bold type** to form a contraction.

Write the contraction on the line.

Then color the part of the cave that matches the sentence.

1. **They will** walk through the opening into the cave. _____

2. **She will** move carefully down the path._____

3. **I have** just found a stalagmite on the floor of the cavern._____

4. We expect **you will** see some bats hanging in the corners._____

5. **Do not** forget to carry two lights at all times. _____

6. **You would** be smart to wear a helmet into the cave._____

7. **We will** count the stalactites hanging from the ceiling._____

8. **It is** always good to see the light again when you leave the cave. _____

Name _____

Contractions

Alaska Camp Out

Adventure # 32

Set up your tent in the wild wilderness of Alaska!
Catch fresh salmon every morning!
Watch out for the grizzly bears. They'll be fishing, too.

1. Add a word from the woodpile to form a compound word on each tent.

2. Then write 10 more compound words made from words in the woodpile. You can use words in more than one compound word.

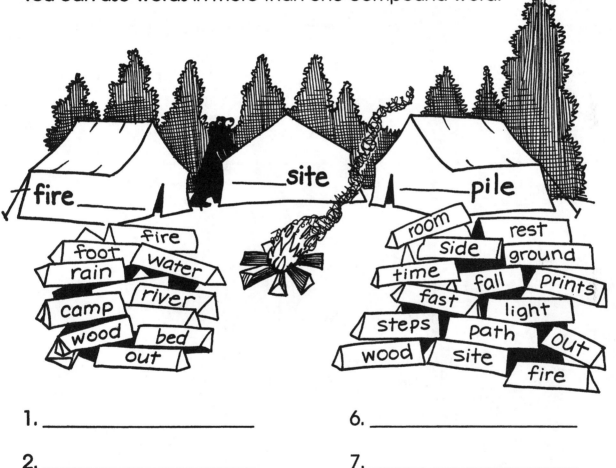

1. _____

2. _____

3. _____

4. _____

5. _____

6. _____

7. _____

8. _____

9. _____

10. _____

Name _____

The Wild Boar Chase

1. Chase the wild boar through the maze of words.
2. Color only the spaces with words that are spelled correctly.
3. Then write the numbered letters on the lines at the bottom to find the name of some things in Borneo that are very large.

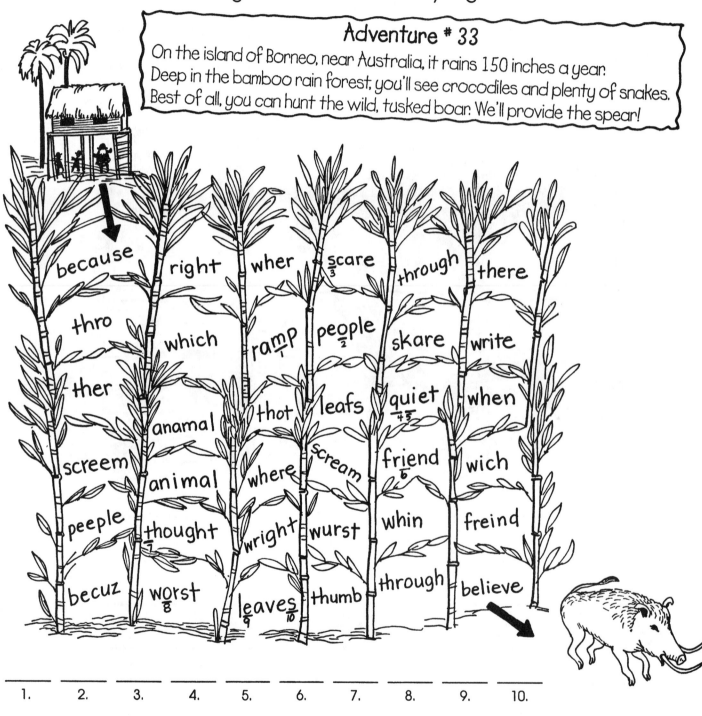

Adventure # 33
On the island of Borneo, near Australia, it rains 150 inches a year. Deep in the bamboo rain forest, you'll see crocodiles and plenty of snakes. Best of all, you can hunt the wild, tusked boar. We'll provide the spear!

because
thro
ther
screem
peeple
becuz

right
which
anamal
animal
thought
worst

wher
ramp
thot
where
wright
leaves

scare
people
leafs
scream
wurst
thumb

through
skare
quiet
friend
whin
through

there
write
when
wich
freind
believe

___ ___ ___ ___ ___ ___ ___ ___ ___ ___
1.   2.   3.   4.   5.   6.   7.   8.   9.   10.

Name _____

Similar Words • Spelling

Copyright ©1998 by Incentive Publications, Inc., Nashville, TN.
Basic Skills/Phonics & Word Skills 2-3

A Lot of Hot Air

Adventure # 34
Rise high above the Earth in a hot air balloon. Float along and see wonderful sights! Watch out for birds!

The balloon is decorated with homonyms.

Homonyms are words that sound the same but are spelled differently.

1. Choose a homonym from the balloon to write in each blank.

2. Circle the homonym that you choose.

3. Then color the design on the balloon.

1. I _____ my hands when I watch the balloon go up so high!

2. While I waited for my turn, I _____ my whole lunch.

3. The _____ was the best part of my lunch.

4. Would it be hard work to _____ designs on the balloon?

5. Will we _____ over the _____ today.

6. We'll enjoy the fresh _____ of the air, _____.

7. I'll _____ postcards while I float through the air.

8. I heard the wind _____ one balloon very fast yesterday.

Name _____

Ski the Alps

Adventure # 35
The Alps have the best skiing in the world! Wax your skis and get ready for some beautiful sights!

The answers to the mountain puzzle are all homonyms.

Homonyms sound alike, but do not look alike.

One word in each clue sentence is the wrong homonym.

Write the correct homonym into the puzzle.

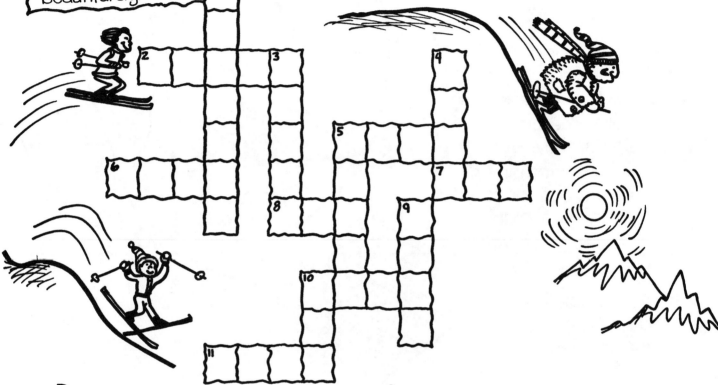

Down

1. The king rained for twenty years.
3. Good shoppers always look for sails.
4. The wind blue down a tree.
5. Let's take a ride in a plain.
9. "Please come hear."
10. This morning there was do on the grass.

Across

2. I have ten pears of socks.
5. She will pair the potatoes.
6. The storyteller told a tall tail.
7. Which weigh do we go?
8. She rowed her boat in the see.
10. I sent a letter to my deer aunt.
11. They new the truth.

Name _____

Copyright ©1998 by Incentive Publications, Inc., Nashville, TN.
Basic Skills/Phonics & Word Skills 2-3

Track the Mountain Gorilla

Proper nouns name special people, places, or things.

They start with capital letters.

Circle the proper nouns that should be capitalized.

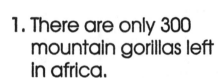

Adventure # 36
A mountain gorilla is not easy to find.
It is a member of an endangered species.
We'll take you to a place where you can track one down (just to look at).
Then we'll search around the world for other endangered species.

1. There are only 300 mountain gorillas left in africa.

2. A scientist named dr. kenwick studies endangered animals.

3. The city of ashland, oregon, is the home of the national forensic laboratory where scientists work to protect endangered animals.

4. Many species of birds in new zealand are endangered.

5. On saturday we'll go to the library to read about the spanish lynx.

6. During the month of april we will travel to mexico to see more animals.

7. We'll return to the united states to visit the florida panther.

Name _____

Proper Nouns

Elephant Ride

The elephant is filled with nouns (names of things).

Plural nouns name more than one of something.

Most names are made plural by adding **s**.

If a noun ends in **sh, ss, ch, z,** or **x**, add **es** to make it plural.

Add **s** or **es** to make these words plural.

If you add **s**, color the section **gray**.

If you add **es**, color it **any other color**.

toe ___

zebra ___

elephant ___

bee ___

dish ___

wish ___

fox ___

box ___

branch ___

lunch ___

bird ___

glass ___

cat ___

kid ___

lion ___

car ___

doll ___

star ___

book ___

Adventure # 37
A ride on an elephant is slow and wobbly. Join the trip to India for elephant rides and other adventures.

Name _____

Plural Nouns

Basic Skills/Phonics & Word Skills 2-3

Visit the Crowded Sahara

We write the animal's name in a special way to show that it owns something.

This makes the name a **possessive noun.**

Add **'s** to each animal's name to show that something belongs to it.

Adventure # 38

It's the largest desert in the world! You see open spaces for hundreds of miles. But if you look closely, you will see that it is filled with animals. Come meet some of the interesting animals of the Sahara!

1. The desert scorpion _____ sting is as poisonous as the bite of a cobra.

2. The sand cat _____ paws have thick fur under its feet to keep it from sinking into the soft sand.

3. A prickly desert hedgehog _____ favorite meal is a scorpion after it bites off the stinger in its tail.

4. The jerboa _____ jump can cover eight feet in a single bound.

5. The addax _____ hooves are wide so it can travel quickly over the soft sand.

6. The chameleon _____ long, sticky tongue allows it to catch insects easily.

7. A male sandgrouse _____ trick for feeding its young is to sit in water until his belly feathers are soaked to the skin. Then the chicks drink from his feathers.

8. The vulture _____ job is to clean up dead animals.

You might want to take notes on these wild and crazy guys!

Name _____

Possessive Nouns

Catch a Great Wave!

Here's how to catch a great wave.
Look at the word each surfer is saying.
Then write three synonyms for that
word in the "talk balloons."

Synonyms are words
that mean the
same thing!

Great!

Huge!

Scared!

1.
2.
3.
4.
5.
6.
7.
8.
9.

Name _____

Catch a Giraffe Ride

WORDS

1. tall
2. thin
3. happy
4. dirty
5. together
6. dangerous
7. top
8. weak
9. young
10. close

OPPOSITES

1. _____
2. _____
3. _____
4. _____
5. _____
6. _____
7. _____
8. _____
9. _____
10. _____

The young giraffe wonders if you can think of opposites **(antonyms)** for all these words.

Each time you write an opposite, color a spot on the giraffe.

Name _____

Antonyms

Galaxy Cruising

Adventure # 41

Cruise the galaxy in our deluxe star cruiser.
See all the planets! Search for new stars!
Look for black holes and wormholes!
Look out for meteors and asteroids!

Connect pairs of stars that are **synonyms** (same meaning). Color them yellow.

Connect pairs of stars that are **antonyms** (opposites). Color them red.

bright

exciting

sparkle

quick

new

boring

chilly

distant

fast

return

trip

journey

darkness

cold

daylight

leave

watch

old

close

Gork !

brilliant

look

The Adventure Company
SPACE CRAFT

Hi!

twinkle

Name _____

Synonyms & Antonyms

Basic Skills/Phonics & Word Skills 2-3

A Scuba Lesson

Adventure # 42

First we'll teach you how to scuba dive.
Then you can come with us to enjoy the undersea world.
Bring your waterproof camera!

Some words have more than one meaning.
Choose a word from the shells that fits both
meanings for each of these.

_____1. the motion of water
to move a hand back and forth

_____2. to drop down to the bottom
a place in the kitchen for
washing dishes

_____3. the land next to the sea
to move without power

_____4. something bright in the night sky
an important person in a movie or play

_____5. to press something into a tight place
a spread made from sweet fruit

_____6. a small bit of water
to let something fall down

drop

play

coast

wave

trunk

land

run

jam

star

sink

We're searching for a blood starfish.
If you find it, color it red.

Name _____

Hike the Great Wall

Look at the groups of words along the wall.

What do the words within each group have in common?

Write a label that describes the words in the group.

Write the labels in the boxes below the word groups.

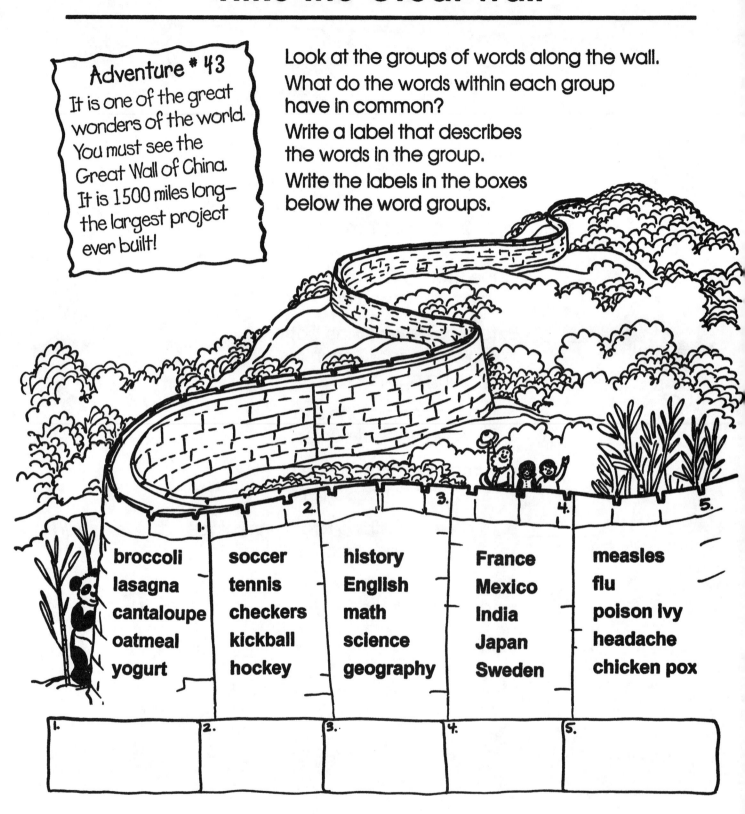

1.
broccoli
lasagna
cantaloupe
oatmeal
yogurt

2.
soccer
tennis
checkers
kickball
hockey

3.
history
English
math
science
geography

4.
France
Mexico
India
Japan
Sweden

5.
measles
flu
poison ivy
headache
chicken pox

1.

2.

3.

4.

5.

Name _____

Word Classification

Copyright ©1998 by Incentive Publications, Inc., Nashville, TN.
Basic Skills/Phonics & Word Skills 2-3

Earthquake Inspection

crust
shockwave
fault
emergency
tremor
seismograph
magma

landslide
plates
disaster
tsunami
aftershock
fire

Find these earthquake words in the puzzle. Circle them and read them.

Ask a teacher or parent to help you find out what they mean.

(Words may be found reading up, down, forwards, backwards, or diagonally!)

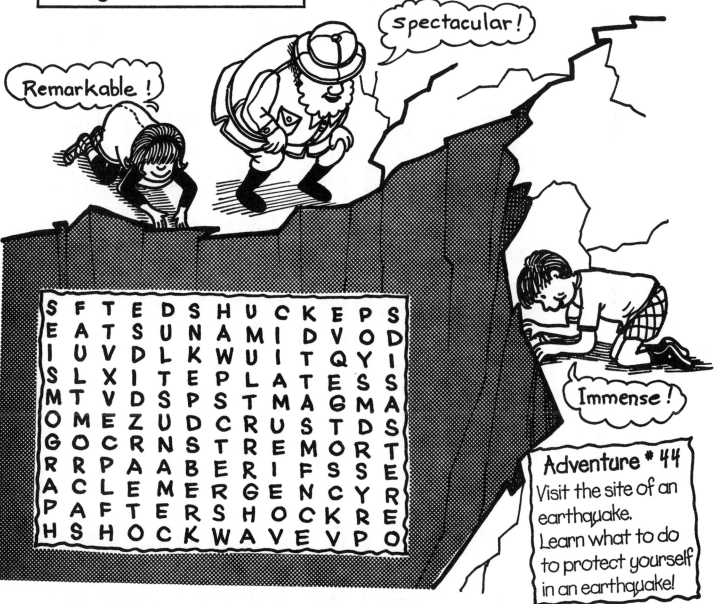

Adventure # 44
Visit the site of an earthquake. Learn what to do to protect yourself in an earthquake!

Name _____

Copyright ©1998 by Incentive Publications, Inc., Nashville, TN.
Basic Skills/Phonics & Word Skills 2-3

New Vocabulary

Hot Spots & Cold Spots

Adventure # 45
Get packed to visit the hottest and coldest spots on Earth. We'll take you to both! Which place would you like to visit first?

Collect some "hot" words and "cold" words.
There are a few to get you started.
You write the rest!

The hottest temperature measured, on a desert in North Africa, is 136°F !

The coldest temperature recorded is −127°F in Vostok, Antarctica.

Hot

steamy
sweaty
broil
humid

_____
_____
_____
_____
_____
_____
_____

Cold

winter
shiver
frosty
blizzard

_____
_____
_____
_____
_____
_____
_____

Name _____

Time Travel

Did you know that the word dinosaur means terrifying lizard?

POP

The Adventure Company
Time Machine

Adventure # 46
No other adventure company offers this trip!
Take a ride in our amazing time machine.
Go back in time to the days of dinosaurs.
See the Tyrannosaurus rex alive—for yourself!

Now that you've run into the greatest dinosaur of all time, why don't you borrow its name for a while?
Write at least 18 words that use letters from this name.
You might be able to make many more!

TYRANNOSAURUS REX

1. _____

2. _____

3. _____

4. _____

5. _____

6. _____

7. _____

8. _____

9. _____

10. _____

11. _____

12. _____

13. _____

14. _____

15. _____

16. _____

17. _____

18. _____

Name _____

Word Formation

Phonics & Word Skills Test

Write the consonants that are missing from the beginning, middle, and end of each of these words.

1. __ a __ e __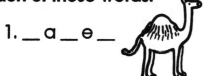

3. __ i __ ar __

5. __ i __ e __

2. __ a __ o __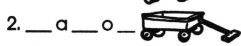

4. __ a __ __ e __

Write the missing consonant blend at the beginning of each word.

6. _____easure _____est

7. _____agon

8. ___aceship

Write the missing consonant blend at the end of each word.

9. du____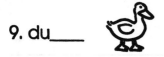

11. bu____

13. sta_____

10. swi____

12. bran____

14. Circle the double consonants in each of these words.

    yellow   rabbit   middle   mess   balloon

15. Circle the words that have a silent letter.

    thumb   plum   comb   wrong   win   ghost

16. Circle the words where **y** is a consonant.

    yes   funny   lady   yolk   yodel   monkey

17. Circle the words where **y** is a vowel.

    yelled   silly   myself   you   Monday   money

Name _____

18. Number these words in alphabetical order:

___ bat

___ boat

___ bite

___ black

___ butter

19. Number these words in alphabetical order:

___ snorkel

___ rhinoceros

___ dinosaur

___ iceberg

___ treasure

___ lion

Write the missing vowels in the spaces.

20.

t _ r n _ d _

21.

v _ l c _ n _

22.

f _ r _

23.

b _ _ t

24. Circle the words with short vowel sounds.

throat   witch   shut   smile   whistle   thunder

25. Circle the words with long vowel sounds.

trouble   groan   right   wrinkle   starve   late

26. Circle the words that have the same vowel sound as **ow** in **clown.**

frown   cloud   flow   growth   mouth   loud

Put the missing ending on each word. Use ing **or** ed.

27. We paddl____ our canoe between the icebergs.

28. It was fun try_____ to find Bigfoot.

29. We should have been watch_____ the dragon more carefully!

30. It's a good thing the helicopter land____ safely in the hurricane.

31. Circle the prefix in each word.

rewrite   disappointment   unhappiness   mistake   impossible

Name _____

Phonics & Word Skills Test

32. Circle the suffix in each word.

unfriendly   dangerous   homeless   drinkable   excitement

Write the root word for each of these words.

_____33. happiness

_____34. strangest

_____35. undrinkable

_____36. hopeless

_____37. disappear

38. Circle the pictures whose names have a long vowel sound.

39. Circle the pictures whose names have a short vowel sound.

40. Circle the pictures whose names have a long vowel sound with a **silent e** at the end.

41. Write the number of syllables next to each word.

____ iceberg   ____ alligator   ____ elephant   ____ hurricane

____ rhinoceros   ____ crocodile   ____ tornado   ____ helicopter

42. Draw a line to match each pair of synonyms.

chilly	terrible
easy	angry
mad	hard
awful	simple
difficult	frosty

Name _____

43. The pictures show three different meanings of one word.
    Write the word.   tr_____

44. The pictures show two different meanings of one word.
    Write the word.   b_____

45. The pictures show two different meanings of one word.
    Write the word.   b_____

46. Draw a line to match the antonyms (opposites).

    beginning   always
    late   happy
    interesting   full
    empty   boring
    never   early
    grumpy   ending

47. Add a word to make these each into a compound word.

    _____fly   camp_____

    school_____   _____ball

48. Add **s** or **es** to make each noun plural.

    box_____   elephant_____   bush_____

    lunch_____   scorpion_____   glass_____

49. Add **'s** to show that each animal owns something.
    the gorilla_____ teeth   Bigfoot_____ footprints   the giraffe_____ spots

50. Circle the words that are proper nouns. Underline the letters that should
    be capitalized.
    texas   september   school   halloween   tuesday

              grandmother   red   monkey

Name _____

Phonics & Word Skills Test

Answer Key

Skills Test

1. c, m, l
2. w, g ,n
3. l, z, d
4. b, rr, l
5. t, g, r
6. tr, ch
7. dr
8. sp
9. ck
10. ng
11. sh
12. ch
13. mp
14. ll, bb, dd, ss, ll
15. thumb, comb, wrong, ghost
16. yes, yolk, yodel
17. silly, myself, Monday, money
18. 1, 4, 2, 3, 5
19. 5, 4, 1, 2, 6, 3
20. o, a, o
21. o, a, o
22. i, e
23. o, a
24. witch, shut, whistle, thunder
25. groan, right, late
26. frown, cloud, mouth, loud
27. ed
28. ing
29. ing
30. ed
31. re, dis, un, mis, im
32. ly, ous, less, able, ment
33. happy
34. strange
35. drink
36. hope
37. appear
38. Circle snake and lion.
39. Circle bird, fish, crab, and tent.
40. Circle rose, cake, nose, and bike.
41. iceberg 2, rhinoceros 4, alligator 4, crocodile 3, elephant 3, tornado 3, hurricane 3, helicopter 4
42. chilly-frosty, easy-simple, mad-angry, awful-terrible, difficult-hard
43. trunk
44. bow
45. bat
46. beginning-ending, late-early, interesting-boring, empty-full, never-always, grumpy-happy
47. Answers will vary.
48. boxes, lunches, elephants, scorpions, bushes, glasses
49. 's added to all three
50. Circle: texas, september, halloween, tuesday. Underline: t in texas, s in september, h in halloween, and t in tuesday

Skills Exercises

page 10–11

10—There are many beginning and ending consonants and blends in these phrases. See that student has circled at least one beginning and one ending consonant or blend in each phrase.

11—There are many middle consonants in these phrases. See that student has circled at least one in each phrase.

page 12

camel	m
riding	d
fuzzy	zz
settle	tt
sinking	nk
clothing	th
desert	s
freezing	z
rodent	d
burrows	rr
viper	p
largest	rg

page 13

lizard follows path: tricky, trade, treat, tree, trap, track, train, try, trouble, trim
snake follows path: start, stork, stone, sticky, sty, stormy, strange, stump, stop, stuck, strong
    The lizard has the shortest path.

page 14

1. stick, slick
2. smile
3. scarf
4. swat, squat, scat, slat, spat
5. sniff, stiff, spiff
6. squirrel
7. skate, slate, state
8. spray, stay, sway
9. snail
10. swim, slim, skim
11. spoon, swoon
12. slip, skip, snip
13. skunk, stunk, spunk
14. sleep, sweep, steep
15. smash, slash, squash, stash
16. scoop, snoop, stoop, swoop, sloop
17. swing, sling, sting
18. stop, slop

page 15

1. clown, crown, frown, brown, drown, blown
2. blue, glue, clue, true
3. write, trite
4. bring, cling, fling, wring, sling
5. clog, frog
6. float, bloat, gloat
7. glass, crass, class, brass
8. plain, drain, train, brain
9. slippery
10. crate, plate, slate
11. creek, sleek
12. dry, cry, sly, fry, try, wry, pry
13. slip, clip, trip, flip, drip, blip
14. pride, slide, bride, glide
15. wrong
16. crow, plow, flow, slow, brow, glow
17. slick, prick, trick, click, flick, crick
18. stop, plop, crop, drop, flop, prop, slop

page 16

Blue icebergs: chip, bush, math, chin, thumb, shop, catch, wish, birch, with
Check to see that the path goes near the blue icebergs.
Circle ng endings on wing, sang.
Circle nk ending on mink.

Copyright ©1998 by Incentive Publications, Inc., Nashville, TN.
Basic Skills/Phonics & Word Skills 2-3

Circle ck endings on
   sock, stuck, duck.
Circle lk ending on
   milk.
Circle st beginning
   and ending on
   stuck, worst.
Circle mp ending on
   jump.
Circle sk beginning
   and ending on risk,
   skin, brisk.
Circle sc beginning
   on scale, scoot.

page 17

jump
crash
float
swim
strike
scream
trick
prowl
drink

page 18

Answers may vary
   some.
1. worry
2. sunny
3. chilly
4. cotton
5. giggle
6. wedding
7. funny
8. terrific

page 19

Lines connect to
   draw a hermit
   crab in a shell.

page 20

1. rain
2. jungle
3. parrot
4. banana
5. monkey
6. jaguar
7. canoe
8. leaf
9. vine
10. river
11. anaconda

page 21

Path should follow:
   run, sun, bull, red,

trip, fall, rip, skip,
   hop, mud, flop,
   flick, stop

page 22

Check drawing to
   see that student
   has followed direc-
   tions.
Long vowel sounds
   are:
1. bow, hair
2. smile, face
3. kite, air
4. kite
5. ice, cream, cone
6. nose
7. cape, green
8. rose, each
9. cupcake

page 23

Sections colored:
   tame, drone, rate,
   cage, cake, page,
   stale, smile, dine,
   slope, ate, mate,
   page, cape, June,
   cone, white, rose,
   ape, plate, rage

page 24

These may be written
   in a different
   order.
1. goofy
2. looking
3. moose
4. loose
5. deep
6. woods
7. Look
8. see
9. feet
10. foot
11. needs
12. cool
13. pools
14. food
15. feed
16. toadstools
17. beetles
18. too
19. zoo
20. free
There are 20 different
   words with double
   vowels.

page 25

Words to be circled:
beast
be
related
These
seek
egrets (3 times)
feet
the (10 times)
eat
meal

page 26

Follow path: tow, low,
   know, mow, show,
   grow, snow, flow

page 27

Answers may vary
   some.
1. pain
2. caught
3. friendly
4. deadly
5. out, eat
6. heat
7. meat, moat
8. ouch
9. beat, boat, bait
10. meal, mail
11. poison
12. retreat
13. mouth
14. glue
15. hours, hairs, hears
16. teach, touch
17. about
18. against

page 28

1. playful (ay)
2. Take (a—silent e)
3. afraid (ai)
4. tail (ai)
5. Wave (a—silent e)
6. Aim (ai); straight
   (ai)
7. Hey (ey); away
   (ay)
8. Escape (a—silent
   e); late (a—silent
   e)

page 29

1. boat
2. loud
3. beach
4. rain

page 30

Y as consonant:
yes
yellow
Yeti
yummy
yodeled
yank
yelled
yikes

Y as vowel:
try
snowy
lucky
today
easily
yummy
silly
fly

page 31

walk
knob
stalk
climb
know
crumbs
wrist
plumber
wren
write
lamb
knead
limb
comb

page 32

possible treasures:
teeth
books
shoes
marbles
shells
bottles
coconuts
cookies
mud
laundry
silver
worms
oysters

spoons
sand
gold
bones
candy
diamonds
jewels

page 33
The turtle with ed got the farthest.
1. ing
2. ed
3. ing
4. ed
5. ed or es
6. ing
7. s
8. ed

page 34
1. Pre
2. Re
3. mis
4. pre
5. dis
6. un
7. re
8. re

page 35
1. ible
2. ly
3. less
4. ous
5. ful
6. ish
7. ant; ly
8. ness
9. tion
10. ment

page 36
1. retired
2. restful
3. friendly
4. beautiful
5. restless
6. unhappy
7. disappointed

page 37
1. usual
2. appear
3. poison
4. quiet
5. strange
6. peace
7. large
8. believe
9. cold
10. power

page 38
1. stop
2. danger
3. work
4. agree
5. blame
6. fine
7. neighbor
8. care
9. tame
10. friend

page 39
1-syllable: to, swamp, Don't, fall, out, of, the, You, might, lose, your, hat, in, This, wild, has, teeth, him, would, be, an, we, should, now, want
2-syllables: Welcome, canoe, little, river, Taming, Perhaps, exit, wrestle
3-syllables: Mosquito, explorers, dangerous
4-syllables: alligator
6-syllables: impossibility

page 40
3-syllable words: rapidly, powerful, waterspouts, anywhere, underground, dangerous, tremendous, tornado

page 41
1. isn't
2. Who's
3. couldn't
4. aren't
5. you're
6. shouldn't
7. We'll
8. They're
9. You've
10. We've
11. don't
12. You'll
"Boom" is the word that appears.

page 42
1. They'll
2. She'll
3. I've
4. you'll
5. Don't
6. You'd
7. We'll
8. It's

page 43
Answers will vary.

page 44
Color these areas: because, right, which, ramp, people, scare, through, there, write, when, quiet, friend, scream, where, animal, thought, worst, leaves, thumb, through, believe
Answer to puzzle is: mosquitoes

page 45
1. wring
2. ate
3. pear
4. sew
5. sail, sea
6. scent, too
7. write
8. blew

page 46
Down
1. reigned
3. sales
4. blew
5. plane
9. here
10. dew
Across
2. pairs
5. pare
6. tale
7. way
8. sea
10. dear
11. knew

page 47
1. Africa
2. Dr., Kenwick
3. Ashland, Oregon, National, Forensic, Laboratory
4. New, Zealand
5. Saturday, Spanish
6. April, Mexico
7. United, States, Florida

page 48
All spaces colored gray except: dishes, wishes, foxes, branches, glasses, lunches, boxes

page 49
Add 's to each animal name in 1–8.

page 50
Answers will vary.

page 51
Answers will vary. Check to see that student has written words that do mean the opposite of those in 1–10.

page 52
Synonyms:
bright—brilliant
look—watch
fast—quick
journey—trip
sparkle—twinkle
cold—chilly

Antonyms
old—new
distant—close
daylight—darkness
exciting—boring
return—leave

page 53
1. wave
2. sink
3. coast
4. star
5. jam
6. drop

page 54
1. foods
2. games or sports
3. school subjects
4. countries
5. diseases, illnesses, or sicknesses

page 55
Check to see that all words are circled.

page 56
Answers will vary. Check to see that student has written words that have to do with heat or cold.

page 57
Answers will vary. Check to see that words student writes use the letters provided.